CONTENTS

Chapter 1   2
    The Jews and Anti-Jewish hatred

Chapter 2   4
    The Nazis

Chapter 3   6
    The Holocaust:

Jews in 'the racial state', 1933-1939   6
The War and Nazi policy in occupied Poland, 1939-1942   9
The 'euthanasia campaign'   10

The 'Final Solution'   11
Phase 1 - "Operation Barbarossa"   11
Phase 2 - "The Final Solution in Europe"   12

"Free world" responses to the persecution of the Jews   17
Jewish responses to Nazi persecution   18
Post-War responses to the Holocaust   22

> "The "triumph of reason" during the Enlightenment in the 18th Century and the French Revolution, which proclaimed the Rights of Man, finally gave the Jews "emancipation""

1
THE JEWS AND ANTI-JEWISH HATRED

The Bible tells us that the Jewish people began life in the land we now call Iraq. From there they migrated to the Land of Israel where they set up the first Jewish state. They enjoyed political independence, with one interruption, for several hundred years, but the Jews lost control of their own lives when a revolt against the Romans failed. They fled into exile taking refuge in trading communities established by other fellow Jews around the Mediterranean. This was the origin of the Jewish population of Europe. Its fate for a thousand years was shaped by Christianity - by then the dominant religion.

The early Christians were Jews who saw themselves as a Jewish sect. But to establish their separate identity, the Christians exaggerated the differences between their beliefs and traditional Judaism. Christian propaganda depicted Jews as "Christ-killers", obsessed with money. The Christian stereotype of "the Jew" was an evil, conspiratorial figure. Since Christianity dominated western European culture, it was able to transmit the basic elements of what we call anti-semitism. Once the Church was recognised, it encouraged Kings and Princes to pass laws which singled out Jews. They were forbidden to own land or to engage in most trades. One of the things they could do was moneylending - a practice forbidden to Christians.

For centuries, Jews survived in Europe as a persecuted and despised minority. But they were allowed to live according to their own laws in their own communities. There were frequent anti-Jewish riots and expulsions - but somehow Jewish life flourished. Jews were even invited into Poland in the 13th century to provide the country with merchants.

The Protestant Reformation began the process which led to religious toleration in Europe. The "triumph of reason" during the Enlightenment in the 18th century and the French Revolution, which proclaimed the Rights of Man, finally gave the Jews equality,

TWO THOUSAND YEARS OF JEWISH LIFE IN EUROPE UP TO 1933

Over a period of sixteen centuries, Jews had contributed to the development of modern Germany. Elsewhere in Europe the earliest Jewish communities dated back even further: This map shows the age of those communities in countries which were to come under German rule or influence between 1933 and 1945.

or 'emancipation'. Between 1790 and 1890, the Jews of western Europe were freed from their ghettos and the laws which oppressed them were scrapped. Jews benefited from the French Revolution and all that came with the modern era: the growth of cities, industry and business. With Jewish success came resentments and jealousies. By the 1880's, there were anti-semitic movements and parties in every European country.

Modern anti-semitism claimed to be 'scientifically' based. Anti-semites referred to writings about 'race' to show that Jews had different genes. This was something which – unlike their faith – Jews could not change. Other thinkers misused the ideas of Charles Darwin about the survival of species and suggested that some 'races' were superior to others. They saw a struggle between 'races' for survival and detected a life-and-death battle between Jews and 'Aryans'.

A Nazi youth rally

2
THE NAZIS

In 1919 the National Socialist German Worker's Party, or Nazi Party, was formed to woo workers away from the international, Marxist socialist movement. Adolf Hitler, who had gone from military service to peacetime propaganda work for the army, joined the party and soon rose to lead it. He built up a power base in Munich, Bavaria, and in 1923 attempted a coup. It failed and he was sentenced to a short prison term. While in prison he set out his ideas in "Mein Kampf" (My Struggle).

Hitler saw the whole world in racial and biological terms. The 'Aryans' were the superior 'race' responsible for all civilisation. The Jews were a demonic force, not even human, which conspired to destroy it. He believed in the "Protocols of the Elders of Zion", a forged 19th century document which alleged a Jewish conspiracy

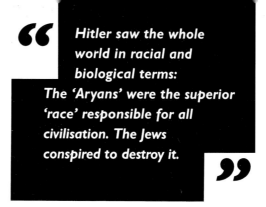

> "Hitler saw the whole world in racial and biological terms: The 'Aryans' were the superior 'race' responsible for all civilisation. The Jews conspired to destroy it."

against the established order. Yet Hitler wanted to transform German society and its people, or "volk", on racial-biological lines. They were to be purified of all so-called weak elements and turned into a 'master race', holding sway over Europe. In particular, they would conquer land in 'the east', meaning Poland and Russia: that way they would gain 'lebensraum' - living space - and also destroy communism, which Hitler saw as a Jewish invention. Mein Kampf was a manifesto for war and destruction.

The Nuremburg Rally in 1934

Only a core of Nazi supporters shared this brutal world vision. Most of the millions of people who voted for Hitler in the elections of 1928, 1930, 1932 and 1933 did so for different reasons. The German Republic founded in 1918 was never popular and Hitler promised to scrap it. He also pledged to overturn the humiliating peace conditions imposed on Germany in 1918, following the First World War. Although the Weimar Republic had achieved stability and prosperity from 1924-1929, the Depression had swept this away. Mass unemployment and the fear of inflation sent voters in search of a saviour.

Hitler was the dynamic leader of a fresh and energetic party. He collected votes from every sector of society, especially the middle-classes. His party militia, the Brownshirts, also attracted thousands of young and unemployed workers. By 1932, the Nazis were the largest single party in the Reichstag - the German Parliament. Anxious to hold on to power and worried by the threat of the communists, Germany's conservative elite offered Hitler the top job - the Chancellorship. Thus, in January 1933 the Nazis came to power quite legally and initially formed a coalition with conservative parties. Then, in February 1933, there was an arson attack on the Reichstag (Parliament). The Nazis said this meant a coup was threatened, and Hitler persuaded a frightened Parliament to give him all the powers of a dictator.

3 THE HOLOCAUST

JEWS IN 'THE RACIAL STATE', 1933-1939

For the Nazis, the persecution of the Jews was the first vital step toward creating a 'racial state'. The goal was a nation pure and strong in racial-biological terms. This goal influenced all social, economic and cultural policy.

In April 1933, after a day long official boycott of Jewish businesses, the Nazis passed laws to turn the Jews into second-class citizens and isolate them from the rest of society. They were forced out of the civil service, legal and medical practice and the educational professions.

© Martin Gilbert 1978

In 1917 Britain promised the Jews a "National Home" in Palestine. But in May 1939, following protest from Egypt, Syria, Yemen, Iraq and the Muslims of India, the British not only introduced severe restrictions on Jewish immigration, but also put pressure on the German, Greek, Yugoslav, Bulgarian and Turkish Governments not to allow "illegal" immigrants into Palestine. As a result of this policy, tens of thousands of Jews lost the chance to reach Palestine, a land in which the League of Nations had specifically given them the right to buy land, to settle on waste land, to till the soil, and to contribute by their own efforts to its economic prosperity. Many of those who were unable to emigrate perished during the Nazi holocaust.

THE DESPERATE SEARCH FOR REFUGE 1933-45

1940 U.S. Congress rejects Bill to open Alaska to Jewish refugees.

1943 British Government rejects the appeal by the Archbishop of Canterbury to abandon the quota system.

1938 At Evian the nations of the world failed to agree on even a *partial* "open door" policy for Jewish refugees. The Australian delegate told the conference: "It will no doubt be appreciated that as we have no racial problem, we are not desirous of importing one".

1940 U.S. State Department rejects Swedish proposal for joint rescue of 20,000 Jewish children from Germany.

1941. US tightens quota system. Congress rejects proposal to admit 20,000 German Jewish children *above* the quota limits.

1937. Severe refugee restrictions introduced.

May 1939. Cuban, Colombian, Chilean and U.S. Governments refuse to admit 900 German Jewish refugees on the "St. Louis". They return to Europe. Many later perished in the Nazi death camps.

1939 - 1945. Jewish immigration limited to 300 a year.

Birobidjan, the "Jewish Autonomous Region" of the Soviet Union, set up in 1934, but *closed* during the war to refugees from European Russia.

- ALASKA
- CANADA 8,000
- UNITED STATES 190,000
- BERMUDA
- MEXICO 2,000
- CUBA 4,500
- DOMINICAN REPUBLIC 705
- VENEZUELA 600
- COLOMBIA
- BRITISH GUIANA
- PERU 500
- BOLIVIA 12,000
- BRAZIL 25,000
- CHILE 14,000
- PARAGUAY 20,000
- URUGUAY 7,000
- ARGENTINA 50,000
- SWEDEN 12,000
- BRITAIN 65,000
- SPAIN 12,000
- PORTUGAL 15,000
- SWITZERLAND 16,000
- SOVIET UNION 250,000
- TURKEY
- PALESTINE 120,000
- EGYPT
- NIGERIA
- KENYA
- TANGANYIKA
- NORTHERN RHODESIA
- ANGOLA
- SOUTHERN RHODESIA
- UNION OF SOUTH AFRICA 8,000
- MAURITIUS 1,750
- CHINA 5,000
- JAPAN 2,000
- Shanghai 25,000
- BRITISH INDIA
- BURMA
- MALAYA
- AUSTRALIA 9,000
- NEW ZEALAND 1,500

January 1939 Anglo-American suggestion that Jewish refugees go to Angola not followed up for fear of offending Portugal.

24 February 1942. The ship "Struma", with 769 Jewish refugees on board, having been refused permission by the British to enter Palestine, and being forced back towards Bulgaria by the Turks, sank in the Bosphorus with the loss of all but one passenger.

1933 - 1935. Unrestricted immigration. Then almost no Jews allowed in from 1936 to 1945.

Jews deported by the British from Palestine while seeking "illegal entry". They were allowed to enter Palestine in 1945.

Some 800,000 Jews, less than one in seven of the Jews murdered, were able to escape from Nazi dominated Europe, or to find refuge in other lands. Their escape was often hampered because no country would take them in. Many countries, some, like India, with large areas of empty land, refused to allow more than a few families to enter.

Shanghai accepted more Jewish refugees than those taken in by Canada, Australia, New Zealand, South Africa and India combined.

The United States and Britain, while allowing in a fairly large number of refugees, maintained strict quota systems which excluded many more.

5,000 visas issued by the Dominican Republic enabled many Jews to escape death by using the visas to go elsewhere.

- ■ Under German occupation or control by December 1941. Home of 8 million Jews
- ▨ Some of the countries almost entirely closed to Jewish refugees. Despite the Conference held at Evian, France, in 1938, and despite the German conquest of much of Europe from 1939 to 1942, refugee quotas were almost everywhere rigidly maintained. As the killing of Jews continued, and following church and humanitarian pressures, an Anglo-American Conference on Refugees was held in Bermuda in April 1943. Its report, published 8 months later, led to *no* relaxation of the world's anti-refugee policies.
- ☐ Approximate number of Jewish refugees allowed to enter 1933-1945. (Shanghai alone required no visa).

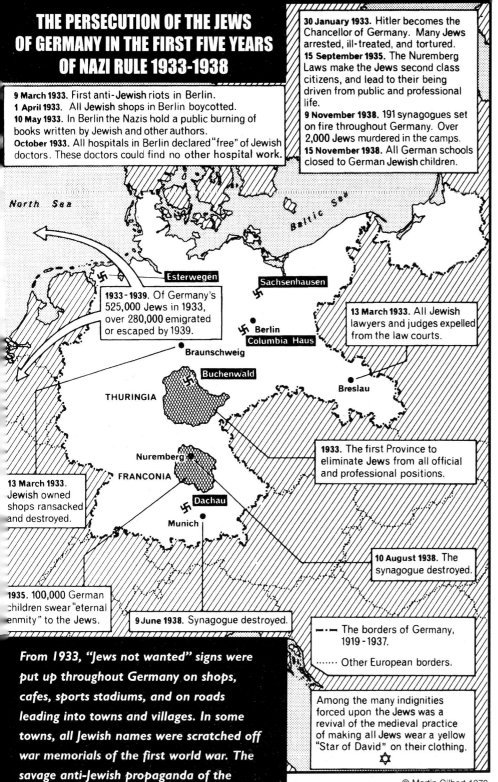

THE PERSECUTION OF THE JEWS OF GERMANY IN THE FIRST FIVE YEARS OF NAZI RULE 1933-1938

9 March 1933. First anti-Jewish riots in Berlin.
1 April 1933. All Jewish shops in Berlin boycotted.
10 May 1933. In Berlin the Nazis hold a public burning of books written by Jewish and other authors.
October 1933. All hospitals in Berlin declared "free" of Jewish doctors. These doctors could find no other hospital work.

30 January 1933. Hitler becomes the Chancellor of Germany. Many Jews arrested, ill-treated, and tortured.
15 September 1935. The Nuremberg Laws make the Jews second class citizens, and lead to their being driven from public and professional life.
9 November 1938. 191 synagogues set on fire throughout Germany. Over 2,000 Jews murdered in the camps.
15 November 1938. All German schools closed to German Jewish children.

1933-1939. Of Germany's 525,000 Jews in 1933, over 280,000 emigrated or escaped by 1939.

13 March 1933. All Jewish lawyers and judges expelled from the law courts.

1933. The first Province to eliminate Jews from all official and professional positions.

13 March 1933. Jewish owned shops ransacked and destroyed.

10 August 1938. The synagogue destroyed.

1935. 100,000 German children swear "eternal enmity" to the Jews.

9 June 1938. Synagogue destroyed.

— · — The borders of Germany, 1919-1937.
······ Other European borders.

Among the many indignities forced upon the Jews was a revival of the medieval practice of making all Jews wear a yellow "Star of David" on their clothing.

> By 1939, committees of doctors, psychiatrists and lawyers had supervised the forced sterilization of 320-350,000 people or one percent of the entire German population.

From 1933, "Jews not wanted" signs were put up throughout Germany on shops, cafes, sports stadiums, and on roads leading into towns and villages. In some towns, all Jewish names were scratched off war memorials of the first world war. The savage anti-Jewish propaganda of the "Stürmer" magazine was in public display cases, and within six years, the 2000 year-old Jewish community was turned into a community of outlaws who could expect nothing but harassment and persecution.

卐 Concentration camps set up on German soil by 1938

© Martin Gilbert 1978

From January 1933, concentration camps were set up to tyrannise all opponents of Nazi policy. Later, the June 1933 'law on unemployment and breeding' forced women back into the home. The July 1933 'law for the prevention of hereditarily diseased progeny' made it compulsory for the physically disabled or 'feeble minded' to be sterilized. By 1939, committees of doctors, psychiatrists and lawyers had supervised the forced sterilization of 320-350,000 people or one percent of the entire German population. They employed mass production techniques such as sterilization by X-rays – techniques that were later used in concentration camps. Nazi persecution of the Jews paused in 1934 due to internal political struggles and foreign policy considerations. But in 1935 these restraints were removed. In September 1935, Hitler responded to pressure from his supporters and ordered the drafting of race laws.

A Synagogue set alight during Kristallnacht on 9th November 1938

The Nuremberg Law for the Protection of German Blood and Honour crudely defined Jews according to the number of their Jewish grandparents. 'Aryans' were prohibited from sexual relations with Jews, and also with Gypsies and Blacks. Jews were stripped of citizenship and increasingly isolated. The Nazis had established an apartheid state.

In 1936 the pace of oppression slowed due to the Berlin Olympics and more diplomatic activity. Then, in 1937, the last restraining forces on Hitler were removed. The 'aryanization of Jewish businesses' – the forced sale of Jewish property at ludicrously low prices – was speeded up. This policy turned Jews into paupers and tens of thousands of them fled from Germany.

From March 1938 Nazi Jewish policy stepped up a gear. That month Germany annexed Austria and within a few weeks Austrian Jews were subjected to the same laws which had accumulated against German Jews over five years. The SS, the special force originally set up as Hitler's personal bodyguard, now gained control of anti-Jewish policy. The SS, controlled by Heinrich Himmler, were fanatical anti-semites. In the autumn of 1938, Polish Jews living in Germany were expelled. The Polish government refused to take them in, so they sat in no-man's-land in miserable conditions. A Polish Jew in Paris, Herzyl Greenspan, whose parents were victims of this policy, was so enraged he assassinated a German embassy official called Ernst vom Rath.

This act provided the excuse for a wave of vandalism and violence against German Jews on 9-10 November 1938. The Nazis called that night Kristallnacht – The Night of Broken Glass. Over ninety Jews were killed and 30,000 rounded up and sent to concentration camps. Few Germans intervened to help the Jews: the Nazis noted this silence and apathy, and knew they could do worse - and get away with it. Kristallnacht was followed by further savage laws aimed at isolating and impoverishing the Jews. Thousands clamoured to escape Germany to whatever country would have them.

Between 1933 and 1939, about half the German Jewish population and more than two-thirds of Austrian Jews (1938-1939) fled Nazi persecution. They emigrated mainly to Palestine, the United States, Britain, Latin America, the Chinese city of Shanghai (which required no visa for entry), and eastern and western Europe (where many would be caught again in the Nazi net during the war). Jews who remained under Nazi rule were either unwilling to uproot themselves, or unable to obtain visas, sponsors in host countries, or funds for emigration. Most foreign countries, including the United States, Canada, Britain and France were unwilling to admit large numbers of refugees.

THE WAR AND NAZI POLICY IN OCCUPIED POLAND, 1939-1942

In September 1939, Germany and Russia carved up Poland between them. At the time, three million Jews lived there. Although there were isolated massacres by SS units, there was no systematic attack on Polish Jews. But the Nazis evicted Jews from areas of Poland which they annexed and sent thousands to an experimental 'Jewish reserve', near Lublin where many perished. After the Germans conquered France, they explored the idea of shipping Europe's Jews to the island of Madagascar. This plan never left the drawing board.

During Spring 1940, the Nazis plundered and isolated the 1.5 million Polish Jews they ruled over, before herding them into 'ghettos'. The method was always the same. In each city with a Jewish population, such as Warsaw, Lodz, Cracow and Lublin, they set up a Judenrat - Jewish Council. Then they registered Jews and their property. Next they confiscated their property and forced the Jews into designated areas. Crammed into these specially designated ghettos, the Jews were prey to disease and starvation. The old, sick and poor were hit first. From January 1941 to July 1942 about 500,000 Jews died of sickness or malnutrition in the Polish ghettos.

> **From January 1941 to July 1942 about 500,000 Jews died of sickness or malnutrition in the Polish ghettos**

In early 1941, the Germans saw another way of exploiting Jews: they agreed to let them obtain food and medicines in return for money, gold and products, and the Jews turned the ghettos into production centres. They believed they would be safe if they produced goods which the Germans needed for their war effort. Indeed, the situation in the ghettos did stabilise during 1941 and it seemed as if the worst might be over. The situation was transformed in mid-1942 due to a further sharpening of anti-Jewish policy.

A child in the Warsaw ghetto

THE 'EUTHANASIA CAMPAIGN'

From September 1939 to August 1941, over 70,000 German inmates of sanatoria – homes for the incurably ill or the disabled – were murdered in gas chambers at five killing centres in Germany and Austria. The murder campaign was organised from Tiergarten Strasse 4, an address in Central Berlin, and was codenamed T4. It was implemented by lawyers and doctors, on Hitler's direct orders. Operation T4 was poorly disguised. There were protests by distressed relatives and by doctors who didn't like the disappearance of their patients. Eventually, the Catholic Church took up the protests. Afraid of alienating opinion at a time of war, Hitler ordered the project to be temporarily discontinued inside Germany, though not for children. But the redundant practitioners of T4 soon found new murderous work elsewhere.

THE 'FINAL SOLUTION'

PHASE 1 - OPERATION BARBAROSSA

'Operation Barbarossa', the invasion of Russia in June 1941, was planned from the beginning as 'an ideological war of extermination'. Einsatzgruppen - mobile SS killing units - got a free hand from the army to execute Soviet officials and Jewish communists. Ordinary soldiers were told that they were rooting out the 'racial enemy'.

From the first the mass killing included men, women and children, without distinction. In August - September 1941 the number of victims recorded by the Einsatzgruppen jumped, as the units started to annihilate whole communities. The SS commanders had waited to see how the army and the local population would react to the massacres. There were no army protests. Moreover, the locals showed enthusiasm to join in the killings, especially in the Baltic, Ukraine and areas adjacent to Romania. Under the conditions of total war and total tyranny anyone who objected could be shot. Knowing this Himmler ordered in more SS killing units. The numbers dedicated to carrying out mass murder rose from the initial force of 4,000 to 40,000 including German police battalions and local militias.

By the end of 1941, about 440,000 Jews had been shot dead. The pattern of these killing operations was usually the same: Jewish men in a city, town or village were rounded up, marched off to a nearby forest, forced to dig mass graves and then shot. But killing in this way was slow and messy. Also, the Jewish populations of centres such as Vilna, Kovno, Bialystok and Minsk were too large to kill all at once using these techniques. These Jews were forced into ghettos until they could be dealt with later.

Himmler saw the Einsatzgruppen at work in Minsk in August 1941. He demanded something less trying for killers (not the victims) and quicker. The SS commanders turned to the T4 experts.
By December 1941 the T4 personnel had brought mobile gas vans into use for the killing of Jews in Serbia (Yugoslavia), Latvia and Poland. They also planned fixed killing sites in Poland and began to experiment with different types of lethal gas. In autumn of 1941, Russian prisoners-of-war were murdered in Auschwitz concentration camp with Zyklon B gas. It was a test run for what became the largest killing centre in human history.

" By the end of 1941, about 440,000 Jews had been shot dead "

PHASE 2 - THE 'FINAL SOLUTION' IN EUROPE

On 31 July 1941 Hermann Goering, Hitler's designated number two, authorised Reinhard Heydrich, the SS leader responsible for Jewish policy, to implement a 'Total Solution' of the 'Jewish Question'. World war had freed Hitler of all constraints. Euphoric about the victories in Russia in autumn 1941, he nurtured dreams of a 'Jew-free world'.

While experiments were conducted with poisonous gas, orders were sent to construct killing centres in Poland. In October 1941 Hitler permitted the first, highly sensitive deportations of German Jews to 'the East' and in November 1941, Heydrich sent out invitations to a conference to coordinate the European-wide killing programme. Meanwhile, gas vans started work in Chelmno on 8 December 1941, killing the Jews from Lodz and the surrounding towns and villages at a rate of 1,000 a day.

The conference, held in the Wannsee suburb of Berlin, was delayed till 20 January 1942. The minutes, taken by Adolf Eichmann, survived the war. At the meeting, Heydrich announced the policy to 'comb out' the Jews of Europe (including England) from west to east. They would be transported to 'the East', where the fittest would be put to work. Those unable to work would be killed and any who survived the forced labour would also be murdered.

In Spring 1942, the killing moved into full swing. In Poland it was codenamed 'Operation Reinhard'. Death camps were established in isolated locations at Belzec, Sobibor and Treblinka. The concentration camp at Majdanek was also adapted for mass murder. Jews in the ghettos were told they were to be 'resettled in the East' and promised food if they went to the assembly places and boarded the trains peacefully. When this ruse no longer worked, the Judenrat and the Jewish police under its control, were ordered, on pain of death, to supply quotas of Jews on a daily basis for transportation. In this way, the largest centres of Jewish population were destroyed in a matter of months.

Auschwitz-Birkenau death camp

GERMAN OFFICIAL PLANS FOR THE "FINAL SOLUTION", 20 JANUARY 1942

The number of Jews mentioned at the Wannsee Conference, country by country and area by area, for eventual deportation, and subsequent death. More than 14 million people were thus marked out for death.

One of the macabre features of the numerical list of the Jews submitted to the Wannsee Conference was the fact that no figure was given for the Jews of Estonia, merely a brief note that Estonia was 'Free of Jews'. This was true; the 1,000 Estonian Jews who had come under German rule in October 1941 had all been murdered during the three months before the Wannsee Conference.

In December 1941, a month before the Wannsee Conference, the first Nazi extermination camp had already come into operation, at Chelmno, responsible for the mass-murder of Jews, Gypsies and Soviet prisoners of war. After passing through corridors marked 'to the showers' and 'to the doctor', the victims were forced into a large truck which was in fact a gas chamber, where they were killed within a few minutes. By the end of 1944 more than 360,000 Jews had been murdered in Chelmno alone.

The Wannsee Conference also specified the number of Jews in *unconquered* countries for eventual destruction, including 330,000 from Britain, 18,000 from Switzerland, 6,000 from Spain and 4,000 from Ireland.

© Martin Gilbert 1978

In western European countries occupied by the Germans, Jewish councils had been established in Spring 1941. The registration of Jews was sometimes disguised as preparation for labour service; in any case, in wartime, people were used to registering for rations. They were also afraid of the penalties for going 'underground'. So, they registered, telling the Nazis that they were Jews. The process of plunder and concentration soon followed. Jews were forced to wear the yellow star on their clothes. In the summer of 1942 the round-ups started, always with the assistance of the local police. Jews were taken to transit camps such as Drancy in France

Men being taken to the gas chambers at Auschwitz death camp.

and Westerbork in Holland. From there they were sent by train direct to the killing centres: Sobibor, Treblinka and Auschwitz. In Summer 1942, Auschwitz was enlarged from a concentration camp to a killing centre. A second camp set up at Birkenau was equipped with huge purpose-built crematoria and gas chambers.

Around 2.7 million Jews perished during 1942: it was the most intense killing period in the Holocaust. The implementation of this 'Final Solution' relied on the cooperation of the local police and civil service in occupied countries. In the case of Germany's allies; Romania, Slovakia, Croatia and Vichy France, each collaborated in the deportation of Jews to the death camps. Denmark and Bulgaria refused to comply as did Italy and Hungary until they were occupied by Germany. Six killing sites were chosen because of their closeness to rail lines and their location in semi-rural areas, at Belzec, Sobibor, Treblinka, Chelmno, Majdanek and Auschwitz-Birkenau. Chelmno was the first camp in which mass executions were carried out by gas, piped into mobile gas vans; 320,000 people were killed there between December 1941 and March 1943, and June to July 1944. A killing centre using gas vans and later gas chambers operated at Belzec where more than 600,000 people were killed between May 1942 and August 1943.

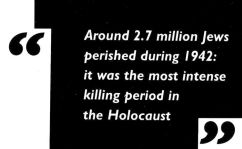

Around 2.7 million Jews perished during 1942: it was the most intense killing period in the Holocaust

Sobibor opened in May 1942 and closed one day after a rebellion of the prisoners on October 14, 1943; up to 200,000 people were killed by gassing. Treblinka opened in July 1942 and closed in November 1943; a revolt by the prisoners in early August 1943 destroyed much of the facility. At least 750,000 people were killed at Treblinka, physically the largest of the killing centres. Almost all of the victims at Chelmno, Belzec, Sobibor and Treblinka were Jews; many thousands were Gypsies. Very few individuals survived these four killing centres, where most victims were murdered immediately after arrival. Auschwitz-Birkenau, which also served as a concentration camp and slave labour camp, became the killing centre where the largest numbers of European Jews and Gypsies were killed. After an experimental gassing there in September 1941 of 250 malnourished and sick Polish prisoners and 600 Russian Prisoners of War (POWs),

THE CONCENTRATION CAMPS

Between 1939 and 1945, six million unarmed and innocent Jewish civilians - men, women, children and babies - were murdered in Nazi-controlled Europe, as part of a deliberate policy to destroy all traces of Jewish life and culture. As many as two million of these were killed in their own towns and villages, some confined in ghettoes where death by slow starvation was a deliberate Nazi policy, others taken to be shot at mass-murder sites near where they lived. The remaining four million Jews were forced from their homes and taken by train to distant concentration camps, where they were murdered by being worked to death, starved to death, beaten to death, shot, or gassed.

Among the hundreds of thousands of *non*-Jews sent by the Nazis to concentration camps were anti-Nazis, Jehovah's Witnesses, homosexuals, the mentally ill, and the chronically sick. In addition, more than 250,000 Gypsies were murdered, in a Nazi attempt to eliminate Gypsies as well as Jews from the map of Europe.

In many of the camps shown here so-called "medical" experiments were carried out, without anaesthetics, solely to satisfy the curiosity and sadism of the doctors. Hundreds of otherwise healthy "patients" were tortured and murdered during these experiments.

🕱 **Auschwitz** concentration camp in which more than 2 *million* people were murdered between 1941 and 1944, including Jews, Gypsies, and Soviet prisoners-of-war.

■ Camps set up solely for the murder of Jews.

🕱 Other camps in which Jews and non-Jews were put to forced labour, starved, tortured, and murdered in conditions of the worst imaginable cruelty. Most of these camps had "satellite" labour camps nearby.

Martin Gilbert 1978

mass murder became a daily routine, more than 1.25 million were killed at Auschwitz-Birkenau, nine out of ten were Jews. In addition, Gypsies, Soviet POWs, and ill prisoners of all nationalities died in the gas chambers. A similar system was implemented at Majdanek, where at least 275,000 people were killed in the gas chambers or died from malnutrition, brutality and disease.

The methods of murder were the same in all the killing centres, which were operated by the SS. The victims arrived in railroad freight cars and passenger trains, mostly from Polish ghettos and camps, but also from almost every other Eastern and Western European Country. On arrival, men were separated from women and children. Prisoners were forced to undress and hand over all valuables. They were then driven naked into the gas chambers, which were disguised as shower rooms, and either carbon monoxide or Zyklon B (a form of crystalline prussic acid, which had been used before the war as an insecticide) was used to asphyxiate them. The minority selected for forced labour were, after initial quarantine, vulnerable to malnutrition, exposure, epidemics, medical experiments and

brutality; many perished as as result. In 1943 the Nazis coined the term Erntefest – Harvest Festival – for the annihilation of the last, remaining Jews of Europe. The Jews of Greece were almost entirely destroyed. The surviving ghettos in Poland and Russia were liquidated and only work camps were left, containing a few thousand Jewish slave labourers. In Autumn 1943 the Operation Reinhardt camps were closed, following revolts in Sobibor and Treblinka.

It became difficult to extract Jews from France, Italy, Romania, and Bulgaria. Yet the killing went on. In March 1944, the German army occupied Hungary, an ally, to prevent it defecting. The 700,000 Hungarian Jews had been protected from the 'Final Solution' until then. Over 437,000 were dispatched to Birkenau between May and June 1944, and only a few thousand were selected to work. During the summer of 1944, once the truth about Auschwitz reached the West, the International Committee of the Red Cross, the Vatican and neutral Sweden intervened actively to save Jews.

However, in the Autumn of 1944 the SS set about liquidating the last ghettos, such as Lodz and Theresienstadt. As the Russian Army approached Auschwitz and other camps in the last months of the war, the Jews were moved westward on 'death marches' which few survived. The remnant, dumped in concentration camps in Western Germany such as Buchenwald, Dachau and Belsen, were finally liberated by allied troops in April-May 1945. Then, with horror, the free world discovered the truth about the 'Final Solution'.

FREE WORLD RESPONSES TO THE PERSECUTION OF THE JEWS

From 1933 to 1938, most western European governments were intent on appeasing, or giving in to, Hitler. They felt guilty about the way Germany had been treated after World War One. Many politicians sympathised with Hitler's anti communism, his social policies and his goals of strengthening Germany. His treatment of the Jews did not figure greatly in their diplomacy.

When Jews started to emigrate from Germany in 1933, most western countries took them in but there were also pressures to restrict the numbers being accepted particularly in countries where there was high unemployment. Efforts to solve the "refugee problem", such as the international conference at Evian in 1938, were too little and too late. After the occupation of Austria in March 1938, and Kristallnacht that November, in addition to the 11,000 Jewish refugees who had already been admitted to Britain from Germany, a further 50,000 including many thousands of children were found a haven under emergency measures. Once war began, Jews were trapped in Europe - and could not get out of German occupied lands; all travel was forbidden and all borders were sealed.

By August 1942 the allies knew the basic elements of the "Final Solution", and there was considerable publicity and protest including broadcasts on the BBC. Others feared that publicity about the mass killings would be dismissed as wartime "atrocity propaganda". In December 1942, the public was informed about the mass murders. There was a wave of outrage and the allies agreed to hold a conference at Bermuda in April 1943, to discuss how to help Jewish refugees. In reality, the opportunities for Jews leaving Nazi controlled Europe at that time were virtually nil and almost all of Poland's 3 million Jews had already been murdered.

Allied action before 1944 was effectively limited to promising retribution for Nazi war criminals. Meanwhile, the war against Germany was proving much more difficult for the Allied armies than they had expected, even after the Normandy landings in June 1944, as the German soldiers fought for every mile, and it was to be ten months before the Allied troops reached the concentration camps of Dachau, Belsen and others.

> *Many politicians sympathised with Hitler's anti-communism, his social policies and his goals of strengthening Germany. His treatment of the Jews did not figure greatly in their diplomacy.*

In the last ten months of the war, allied diplomats were more active in lobbying neutral powers and the Vatican to save Jews where possible. However, even when asked by Jewish organisations, the Allied air forces were never ordered to bomb Auschwitz, which could have stopped the killings at least for a while.

JEWISH RESPONSES TO NAZI PERSECUTION

In the immediate aftermath of the war, Jews were criticised for not having escaped from Europe while they had the chance. It was frequently said that they "went to the gas chambers like sheep to the slaughter". Some commentators even suggested that the Jews collaborated with the Nazis in their own destruction. These views fail to take into account the terrible situation for the Jews, and what little they were capable of doing.

The Jews of Germany could not have known what lay in store for them: annihilating Jews was not one of Hitler's publicly stated goals while he was running for office. Jews believed that Hitler would act more responsibly once he was in power. When the persecution showed no signs of receding, those who could, did emigrate. But this option was only available to the young, those with portable skills, or the wealthy. In any case, there were few countries that would take in Jewish refugees.

Polish Jews responded to the Germans by remembering Jewish history. Jews had been persecuted in the past, but most had survived. They followed the old strategies of bribery, appeasing their oppressors and prayer. They tried not to do anything that would

Barracks at a concentration camp

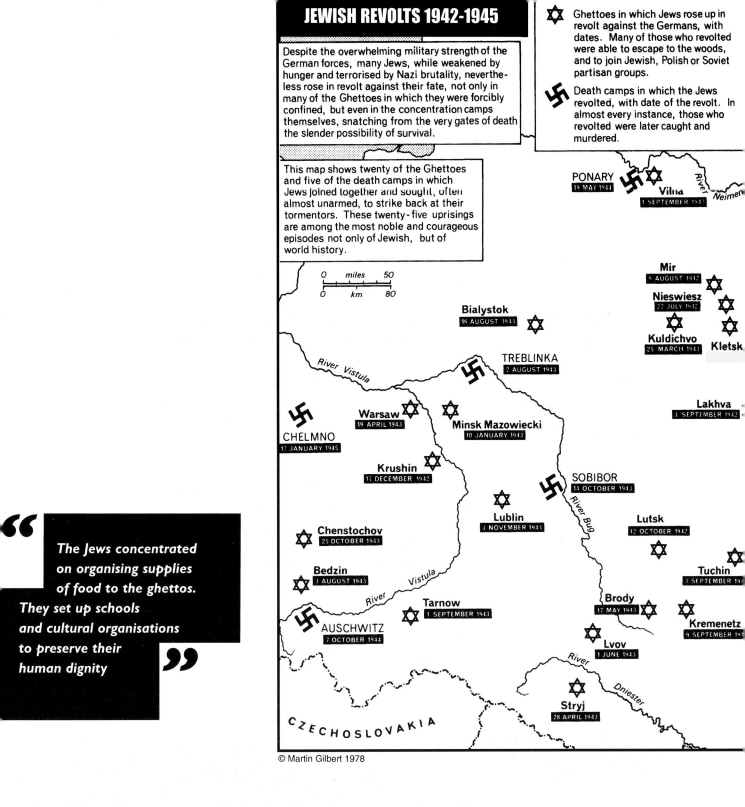

> *The Jews concentrated on organising supplies of food to the ghettos. They set up schools and cultural organisations to preserve their human dignity*

place entire communities at risk. They also knew that they could expect little help from the outside. Relations between Jewish and Christian Poles were very bad, while the allies were far away and on the defensive.

So the Jews concentrated on organising supplies of food to the ghettos, often illegally. They set up schools and cultural organisations to preserve their human dignity. This was itself a form of defiance. They arranged to work for the Germans, thinking that this would ensure their safety. Militant resistance was rare - until the mass deportations began in the summer of 1942.

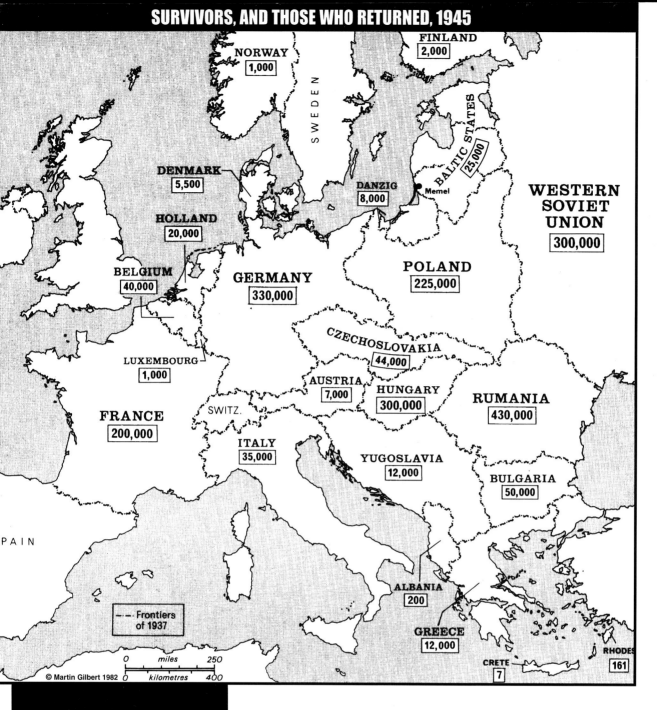

SURVIVORS, AND THOSE WHO RETURNED, 1945

In addition to the 300,000 survivors of the concentration camps, over a million and a half European Jews survived Hitler's efforts to destroy them.

The Jews of the Baltic and Russia, who faced the onslaught of the Einsatzgruppen, had little time to react. Nevertheless, once the initial wave of killings was over, many young Jews organised resistance cells in the ghettos. Often they got help from the community leaders, but there were arguments about the wisdom of armed resistance. Few Jews in the ghettos had military training. Weapons were in pitifully short supply. Attacks on the Germans would lead to reprisals, and the ghetto fighters could not protect the potential victims: the old, the women and children. Only the fit and the young could flee to - or survive in - the forests.

Because of these dilemmas, armed resistance came late and involved only small numbers of Jews. It also depended on the progress of the war. The most intense phase of killing, from June 1941 to late 1942, coincided with the height of Nazi power. Revolts such as that in the Warsaw ghetto in April 1943, were gestures of defiance rather than resistance: the fighters knew they had almost no chance of survival and could not protect their people. Later in the war, Russian Jews were able to escape from their ghettos and join the Red Army partisans.

Yet, paradoxically, the approaching end of the war only strengthened the determination of other Jews, such as those in Lodz, to hang on. The Jewish ghetto leaders agonised over the best approach. None of their options was 'good'. The Nazis had put them in an impossible situation. Some, like Adam Czerniakow in Warsaw, chose suicide rather than co-operation in the deportations. Others, like Chaim Rumkowsi in Lodz, believed that appeasing the Germans and working for them was the best hope of survival. It is very hard, and possibly wrong, for those who did not suffer with them to sit in judgement on them.

> "Revolts such as that in the Warsaw ghetto in April 1943 were gestures of defiance rather than resistance"

Similar patterns emerged in the concentration and death camps. Whereas communists and socialists could rely on resistance networks, the Jews were isolated. Age, gender and skills determined whether a deportee would be selected for work, prior to deportation or on arrival in Birkenau. In Chelmno, Sobibor, Belzec and Treblinka there was only a very small labour force and almost no chance of surviving. (There were only two known survivors from Belzec where 600,000 were murdered). The initial stages of the killing process were cunningly disguised and took under three hours, giving the hungry and exhausted Jews, just pulled off the trains, no time to react or to resist.

Jews from western Europe were deported with relative ease in 1942 because few understood the meaning of 'resettlement in the East'. Once information about the killing centres became more widespread the Nazis found it harder to trap Jews in mass round-ups. In France hundreds of Jews took to the hills with the Maquis, the underground army.

A pile of the victims' glasses at Auschwitz death camp

POST-WAR RESPONSES TO THE HOLOCAUST

Immediately after the war, survivors gathered in Displaced Persons camps. Some wanted to go home, others to leave Europe for America or Palestine. The Jews of Palestine were eager to take them in but were prevented from doing so by the British. The struggle with Britain from 1945-48 over British policy in Palestine, muted British sympathy for the Jews. Attention to the Holocaust was distracted by the birth of Israel and its problems.

Allied troops who liberated Buchenwald concentration camp

The dock at the Nuremburg war crimes trial which began on the 20th November 1945

The shock which followed the liberation of the concentration camps produced only short-lived results. The victorious allied authorities put the surviving top Nazi leaders on trial at Nuremberg in 1945-46. Several thousand individual war criminals were also tracked down and put on trial in Germany or in the countries where they had committed their crimes. However, by 1949 the Cold War between East and West had turned the German people in the western sphere of influence, into potential allies. The German Federal Republic was brought into being and de-Nazification was ended. Many war criminals escaped justice either by fleeing to South America or the Arab world. Others were freed by German courts after serving token sentences.

It was not until the 1960's that a wave of trials re-awakened public awareness of the 'Final Solution'. In 1960 the Israelis captured the top Nazi bureaucrat, Adolf Eichmann, and put him on trial in Jerusalem for crimes against the Jews. In 1963-65, the Germans tried several guards who had served at Auschwitz. In 1974, a German court tried Franz Stangl, commandant of Treblinka, after he had been extradited from South America. Even today, Nazi collaborators are being exposed and put on trial.

> *Even today, Nazi collaborators are being exposed and put on trial*

The first intellectuals to grapple with the implications of the Holocaust were Jewish. Next came Christian theologians who faced the task of explaining the role of God in the Holocaust and the part played by Christianity in fostering anti-semitism.

By the 1970s and 1980s, the Holocaust was being explored in novels, poetry and films. The threat of nuclear war and the recurrence of genocide also caused sociologists and historians to search for the roots of the 'Final Solution' in human behaviour. It was frequently argued that if this could be fathomed then it would be possible to understand how genocide can come about and how it can be prevented.

For a quarter of a century, the Holocaust was essentially the private grief of Jews all over the world. In the last fifteen years it has become a metaphor for evil, a synonym for every kind of genocide, no matter how dissimilar.

The moral, ethical and historical dimensions of the Holocaust remain profoundly relevant – through learning and examining the lessons of the past we may understand how hard it is to construct a decent society, how far we have fallen short of this in the past and why it is essential to keep on striving towards this goal.